What Was It Like Before the Telephone?

Acknowledgments

Executive Editor: Diane Sharpe
Supervising Editor: Stephanie Muller
Design Manager: Sharon Golden
Page Design: Simon Balley Design Associates
Photography: Ancient Art and Architecture Collection: page 10; Mary Evans Photo Library: pages 13, 18-19, 21; Robert Harding: cover (middle right), page 27; Peter Newark's Western Americana: cover (bottom left), page 11; Alex Ramsay: page 17; Ann Ronan Picture Library: cover (top right), pages 8, 15, 25; Science Museum: page 22.

Library of Congress Cataloging-in-Publication Data

Humphrey, Paul, 1952-
     What was it like before the telephone?/Paul Humphrey; illustrated by Lynda Stevens.
       p.   cm. — (Read all about it. Social studies. Level B)
     Includes index.
     ISBN 0-8114-5736-2 Hardcover
     ISBN 0-8114-3781-7 Softcover
     1. Communication and technology — Juvenile literature.   [1. Communication — History.]   I. Stevens, Lynda, ill. II. Title. III. Series: Read all about it (Austin, Tex.). Social studies. Level B.
P96.T42H86 1995
302.2'09—dc20

          94-28402
          CIP
          AC

1 2 3 4 5 6 7 8 9 00 PO 00 99 98 97 96 95 94

STECK-VAUGHN
READ ALL ABOUT IT

What Was It Like Before the Telephone?

Paul Humphrey

Illustrated by

Lynda Stevens

STECK-VAUGHN
C O M P A N Y
ELEMENTARY · SECONDARY · ADULT · LIBRARY

4

This is the communications room. It has many pictures and other things that show us how people sent messages before the telephone was invented.

Come with me, and you'll find out.

7

How do you think people sent messages to each other before they had telephones?

That's right. This picture shows a mail carrier. Hundreds of years ago, he carried letters and packages to people.

I'll bet it took him forever to deliver one letter.

9

People sent messages even before that.
Some used drums to beat out a message.

Some Native Americans used fire to communicate. They sent smoke signals to each other.

I wonder what they are saying.

Those are semaphore towers. People sent messages from one hilltop to another by raising or lowering the tower's arms.

Other people sent messages using semaphore flags.

What happened if it was foggy?

No one could see the message.

That is a carrier pigeon. People would
put a message into that little container on
its leg. Then they would send the bird flying
to the person receiving the message.

15

People wanted to include more in their messages, so they made pens out of feathers. They sharpened the end of one, dipped it in ink, and wrote their message.

How did they
get their message
to the other person?

17

A postal system was started, and letters and packages were carried by stagecoach from one person to another.

18

19

Pony Express riders galloped thousands of miles from one side of the United States to the other.

I would like to have been a Pony Express rider!

It was used for flashing out a message in a code called Morse code.

A long flash is called a dash, and a short flash is called a dot. Does anyone know any Morse code?

Then there was an invention that used electricity to send a Morse code message along wires. This invention was called the telegraph.

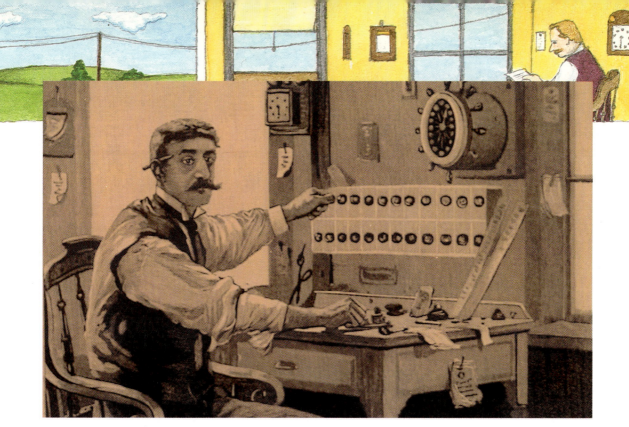

The telegraph operator would tap out a
message on a transmitter like this one.
But you had to be able to read the code.

25

The next invention was a big step forward. It meant that messages could be sent over long distances and that people could talk normally. What was it?

The telephone!

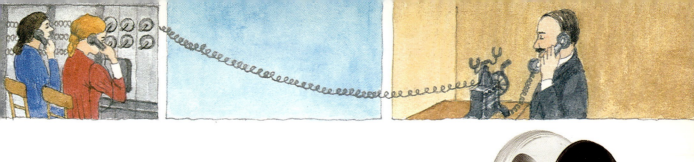

That is one of the first telephones
ever invented.

People have always wanted to send messages to each other. Today we can use the telephone to talk to people all over the world. We can even send a written message instantly using a fax machine.

Can you remember what kind of message each of these things sent? The answers are on the last page, but don't look until you have tried naming everything.

1.

3.

2.

4.

Index

Answers: 1. Writing 2. Semaphore messages 3. Drumbeat 4. Morse code